THE INHABITANT

Poems by Lewis Turco

Prints by Thomas Seawell

with an Introduction by Vern Rutsala

DESPÀ PRESS
BOX 123, NORTHAMPTON, MASSACHUSETTS 01060

ACKNOWLEDGEMENTS

The author and the artist owe acknowledgement and thanks to the Research Foundation of the State University of New York for fellowship aids in support of the writing of this book, and the making of the prints.

We also owe thanks to Robert Steinen of the Art Department of the State University of New York College at Oswego for his photography, from which the reproductions of Mr. Seawell's prints were made.

Thanks are also due the editors and publishers of the following publications for permission to reprint a number of the poems: *American Weave, Antioch Review, Concerning Poetry, December, Kamadhenu, The Miscellany, New England Review, New Orleans Review,* and *Poetry Northwest.*

Also, *Poetry,* for permission to reprint "The Kitchen," "The Scythe," and "The Bedroom," copyright 1969 by The Modern Poetry Association, and *Red Clay Reader 5* for permission to reprint "The Livingroom," copyright 1968 by *Red Clay Reader.*

"The Guestroom" appeared originally in *Southwest Review* under the title "I Speak of an Old Man"; "The Dwelling House" was first published in *The Carleton Miscellany* under the title "Sleep."

The introductory poem "Evenings at Home" by Vern Rutsala was originally published in *The Northwest Review,* copyright 1970, and is here reprinted by permission of the author of the poem.

The prints by Mr. Seawell have been exhibited nationally, in competitive exhibitions and commercial galleries.

All correspondence should be addressed to Despa Press, Box 123, Northampton, Massachusetts 01060

CONTENTS

Introduction by Vern Rutsala   7

THE INHABITANT

The Door   11
The Hallway   13
The Hallseat   14-15
The Attic   17
The Photograph   18-19
The Livingroom   21-22
The Couch   23
The Dining Room   24
The Sideboard   25
The Kitchen   27
The Linen Calendar   28
The Playroom   31-32
The Portrait of a Clown   33
The Study   35
The Cat   36
The Bedroom   39-40
The Pillow   41
The Bathroom   43
The Mirror   44
The Basement   47
The Scythe   48
The Porch   51-52
The Glider   53
The Guestroom   55
The Looking-Glass   56
The Summerhouse   59
The Garden   60
The Dwelling-House   63-64-65

LIST OF PRINTS

The Door 10

Detail from The House — Hallway 12

Detail from The Clock and The Bell 16

Detail from The House — Livingroom — Diningroom ... 20

Detail from The House — Kitchen 26

The Window 30

The Shelves 34

The Bed 38

The Sink 42

Detail from The House — Basement 46

Detail from The House — Porch 50

The Game Closet 54

The Stove 58

The House 62

An Introduction by Vern Rutsala:

EVENINGS AT HOME

After dinner you hear footsteps outside,
        but they all go by on their intricate journeys —
    carrying sealed messages to gas companies,

but with such deference:
        on tiptoe, speaking quietly
    even to house numbers and wagons.

The same politeness shrouds the house, making you
        smile at furniture
    before sitting down to worry about the carpet —

the way it stretches,
        sending pile to every corner — such a flat beached
    fish that only winces when you

step on it, but never whimpers, never even sighs.
        All the objects around you are well-bred, stoic,
    resigned to duties only disaster

will release them from.
        You wait
    for disasters too, some booming

invitation to run in the street, free finally of that
        contract you signed to sit still all the evenings
    of your life.

But some nights you can't stop walking.
> All the chairs point out
> aches, the little bruises thinking brings.

You walk around opening
> and closing doors. Or stare out at
> the faint light on the trees,

thinking
> of minnows.
> You stop at closets, feel the material of

an old life, look at shoes. And you don't speak.
> Not even
> the need to lie squirms in your

throat. You eat the powder of silence
> and wander toward sheets
> stiff as collars,

the drugged journeys of
> heavy-handed dreams,
> or the bright tumor of sleeplessness.

"THE DOOR"

"The Door"   *etching — engraving*

THE DOOR

There is a door
    made of faces
faces snakes and green moss

which to enter is
    death or perhaps
life which to touch is

to sense beyond the
    figures carved in
shades of flesh and emerald

the Inhabitant at home
    in his dark
rooms his hours shadowed or

lamptouched and that door
    must not be
attempted the moss disturbed nor

the coiling lichen approached
    because once opened
the visitor must remain in

that place among the
    Inhabitant's couches and
violets must be that man

in his house cohabiting
    with the dark
wife her daughter or both.

detail from "The House" *Hallway*

THE HALLWAY

The Inhabitant stands in his hallway. A long way from the door, still the gentleman has a distance to go before he can leave, or enter, or simply resume.

Here there is small illumination. The only window is of squares of stained glass, in the door behind him which is closed.

Things wait in the narrow aisle. Objects beguile him — each has its significance, in and beyond itself; each is an obstacle in a way to be touched and passed:

Touched and repassed, and with each touching to become more than the original substance. The Inhabitant stands in his hallway, curiosities looming ahead and behind.

It is as though, almost, this furniture had become organs, extensions of his body. If he listens, the gentleman may find his pulse booming in the hallseat, under the lid, gently, among artifacts and mathoms.

Let him proceed; let his football say *clum,* silence, *clum.* Let the stained light lie amber on a black umbrella in its stand, fall scarlet on the carpet, make a blue haze of a grey hatbrim rising in shadow to the level of his eye to rest on an iron antler in the hall.

The Inhabitant is home. Let him go down the hallway, choosing to pass the stair and banister this time, pass these things of his, levelly, moving from light to light, shadow to shadow.

P. 13, stanza 6, line 1:
"footfall," not "football."

THE HALLSEAT

This is the place where
    no one ever sits
        in halflight

the golden oak fading the
    paper fading behind a
        spotted mirror

like an entrance into flowers
    and trellises an entrance
        for eyes

only the gate guarded by
    two stags on either
        side of

the mirror where only one
    hat ever hangs but
        the true

entrance is there beneath the
    mirror and the mirror's
        stags where

no one ever rests for
    it is a trap
        opening upward

only in the seat itself
    where certain moments repose
        forgotten now

a rose turned to rosedust
    sheet music the dim
        notes rising

off the page songs and
fragrances diminishing and returning
sometimes in

the darkness here in this
passageway always at some
edge of

recall but there is a
volume too in the
hallseat in

which the rose is written
down where music blooms
in silence

waiting for someone to spring
the trap and fall
and stay

to listen to smell the rose
and be written down
like everyone.

THE ATTIC

Things, the work of dust and summer flies, upstairs over the other rooms, lying where they were created under the covers of trunks. The mathoms, original art of shadows drowsing in boxes: dresses and shirts worn by the seasons at their balls and weddings; the toys mice play with; mirrors reflecting upon solitude; cords and scissors.

Downstairs the Inhabitant moves slowly among orderly rooms; his wife is a comfort, his child little trouble, and the cat is kindly for the most part.

In the attic it is quiet; rain touches the roof and falls slowly from the eaves.

If the Inhabitant intrudes at odd times he does not notice the machine amid the clutter. It stands in a corner behind a rack of clothes in shades of brown and yellow, a red flower printing itself now and again on some fabric fading into the slanted beams.

He is mildly surprised by the numbers of mathoms. At times it is hard to remember: a photo in a gilt frame, a ribbon, someone's scroll.

They are worth an hour's musing in semi-darkness, the hum of a wasp on the ceiling, street sounds muffled. The machine is never discovered: the only mechanism to intrude — lightly, nearly beneath any threshold — is a mower in the hands of a distant neighbor.

When the door of the mathom shop is closed and the Inhabitant leaves the print of his footsteps for a moment on the wooden stairs, things pause. There is no movement, not even of time. The mathoms listen until, downstairs, carpets and rugs swallow the noises of living, until the furniture absorbs motion.

Then the machine clicks on: the clock dial begins to turn; dust feeds the cogs. It is making things, making them slowly, out of the debris of afternoons and the streetlamp suicides of evening moths.

It takes forever, but the mathoms accumulate, sift into the corners like drifts, send up an aroma as of the slowest burning — the scent of must. Under the mathom shop the Inhabitant senses — at most, perhaps — a vague weightfulness overhead and, now and then, the cat acts strangely.

THE PHOTOGRAPH

It is unwise
to trap a moment such as this
in a frame gilt or
otherwise for such moments

change at any
rate no trap is strong enough look
she lay ensnared in her
layers of clothing among

utter shades here
in this trunk where nothing has influenced
her but clear glass yet
she has grown older

than old her
youth in its fanciful bows shocks the
memory of greys and wrinkles
this creature is absurd

can never have
existed not in any light of any
day under the sun no
one ever lived in

any time so
antique so suffused with ivory and lavender
the odor of bayberry no
camera was ever as

clearly misty no
lens so oval she inhabits an egg
under glass clearly she is
unborn her maturity a

trap for her
discoverer who falls in love with neverness
from which there is no
escape now that she

has been thus
exhumed he will live with her sharing
guilt now and despair forever
in odd moments peering

through crystal into
laces and shadow the long age of
attics hearing only the hornet's
drone and impossible songs.

THE LIVINGROOM

The chairs of his livingroom lounge thinking in groups. Couches remember what it was like here yesterday and the day before.

Lamps dimly recall old shadows in the various corners. The carpet ruminates, sometimes darkly, but again less so, running out perhaps from under a table.

Two candles counterpoint an African violet, broadleafed in a large pot; their sentinel lances prefigure a grey print in a grey frame behind them on the wall.

The gentleman's chair — gainly in complement beside the grace of a lady's rocker, yet separated from her moods by the sewing cabinet — stands in the far corner, a boy's skull growing out of the cutplush of the fabric of the seat.

The boy's ivory jaw falls and closes. The child is singing.

He listens, the Inhabitant of this room, as his furniture is listening, but the boy is not singing to him, obviously, for he can hear nothing. Yet the chairs are enthralled — even the candles seem to lean in the direction of the skull making silence vocal.

The skull is yellow, and there is yellow thread in a needle which lies on the wood of the sewing cabinet, but the dominant tone of the furniture is brown, as brown as the study into which the Inhabitant has sunken. Why can't he hear what the boy is singing, bone against the upholstery and the ornate arms, the frame of bent dark wood like the oval of an egg?

He watches the skull grow upward on its stem of spine; he waits till it is tall as a lily, and the chairs wait, the couches roar quietly.

If the boy begins to stare at him, what will he do? His hair is thinning, it is true, and he has a slight stomach — yet he is a lover of song; it is not his fault.

Perhaps it would be well to applaud in the thin lamplight, among the uneasy things, the unsettling mood of the livingroom. Perhaps he ought, really, to pretend he had heard, for the skull is now as tall as he himself sitting in the gentleman's chair beside the grace of his lady the rocker, her spine curved now against the stair-corner, not straight as it had been when her bride's body would not bend to the will of a stripling.

Perhaps it would be as well not to listen to the song the couches recall; to forget to applaud might be wiser than to listen to the skull's yellow music which, strangely, now that he has decided, comes moving quietly across his teeth like a shadow to stir the leaves of the violet.

THE COUCH

It waits against
the wall like some
old lion couching in gloom

it is harmless
one can be seated
on its hide and it

will not move
even to take its
repast look one may be

seated here and
one will not disappear
into the plush flowers that

camouflage hunger it
is harmless though famished
in the room on the

carpet which rolls
into the underbrush of
an evening murmurous with crickets.

P. 22, stanza 1, line 3:
"has," not "had heard."

THE DINING ROOM

It is dark in the dining room. A candle studs the shadows.

Beneath the table there is an animal that eats light. The Inhabitant does not know its shape, nor does he know the color of its breath, but its ears listen to wax melting.

There will come a time when the candle shall be small enough to swallow. The Inhabitant waits wondering; the beast bides in darkness.

The Inhabitant remembers the mountains like the teeth of wolves tearing at the sky. The windows of his house are the eyes of kine.

In the mountains there are stars to be eaten, for they are fit prey and are seldom caught. In the umbra of the dining room the Inhabitant fears the animal which is his brother waiting till the feast is over.

He hoards his candle, but may not stop its burning; he fears darkness, but it is his own shadow.

Hungering, he waits in his appetite. Beasts bide at the edges of the room.

THE SIDEBOARD

The monster in
the corner the tame gargoyle kisses
the daily china guards

the stainless service
serves as retainer swallows towels and
sustains this daily bread

till it is
served sets the tone complacent against
the wall which like

the lining of
a belly envelops the hours envelops
the food of hours

heartbeats watchticks pulses
and upon the top shelf of
the corner familiar there

is enshrined an
old heart a windup clock its
pendulum counting meals stainless

service linen and
conversation ruminant browsing continent the familiar
monsters in the corners.

detail from "The House" *Kitchen*

THE KITCHEN

In the kitchen the dishwasher is eating the dishes. The Inhabitant
listens to the current of digestion — porcelain being ground,
silver wearing thin, the hum and bite of the machine.

His wife does not hear it — she is humming, not listening. But the
Inhabitant is aware of movement in the cupboards, of the
veriest motion — the castiron skillet undergoing metamorpho-
sis, perhaps; becoming its name: the wives' *spider* spinning
beneath the counter, weaving and managing, waiting for the
doors to open.

Each cup has it voice, each saucer its ear, and the thin chant planes
between the shelves, touching the timbres of glass and crystal
as it passes. The gentleman listens, is touched to the bone by
this plainsong — he feels his response in the marrow's keening.

But the women do not — neither the elder nor the child — sense the
music their things make. Their lips move, a column of air rises
like steam, and there is something in a minor key sliding along
the wall, touching the face of a plastic clock, disturbing the
linen calendar beside the condiments.

It is as though, the Inhabitant reflects, the women are spinning. It
is as though, while he waits, they weave bindings among the
rooms; as though the strands of tune were elements of a sister-
hood of dishes, the ladies, the spider in the cabinet, even of the
dishwasher, done now with its grinding, which contributes a
new sound — a continuo of satiety — to the grey motet the
kitchen is singing.

THE LINEN CALENDAR

The background hours are
     woven among
the months which hang

upon the wall where
     meals are
taken where the months

trace one another their
     rigid files
and ranks printed upon

brown linen the smell
     of dark
coffee eggs sunnyside sound

of skillets and spiders
     weaving sustenance
as August eats July

September bites October groping
     toward winter
and the new year's

new linen against time's
     green wall
its webs and weavings.

"THE WINDOW"

"The Window"   *etching — engraving*

THE PLAYROOM

Stories are done for the evening. The Inhabitant can tell that she
is remembering that summer's day.

The face of the painted clown muses out of its frame, neither smiling
nor frowning. The furniture, painted in imitation of noonlight,
belies the sunset and reminds her of their outing — the museum,
the exhibits under glass:

There lay the two moose, locked upon love's combat. Everything was
as it had been: the great bulls were dead — so said the placard
upon the glass — thus they were found, silent in the wood,
horns fused.

The object of their contention had vanished by the time men hap-
pened upon the bodies steaming in a spring thaw. The placard
related the fantastic sight: hundreds of yards of woodland
smashed and torn — they had been a long while dying, these
great beasts, one of a broken neck — the lucky one.

Thirst had taken the other bull at length. Yet, even on his side he'd
dug a dozen holes, deep as his hooves could delve, trying for
water.

Despite the bedtime tales, the child remembers. The gentleman
damns that Jack, old Time, the giant killer, damns his eye: the
one that — when the just-so book is closed, winks as he strangles
the three bears beneath the darkled covers.

The Inhabitant says goodnight, sweet dreams of bunnies in a green-
ing copse — forget the moose: they'd had a lovely life, free and
roaming the free mountains, waters falling in the great gorge,

wind in their horns, their loins and lungs bursting with love —
forget the dying moose. Don't you wish that you were a happy
bunny lying in a sea of daisies blooming ever?

And she has answered him in his own words. The Inhabitant had
wondered how long he had been hearing those syllables couching in umbra, the stars winking in at the windows, lying about
where they were in the night by light years and by dark:

"I wish I was nothing." The fool in him asked why — "Because
then nothing could hurt me."

The Inhabitant tells his daughter he would never let the giant killer
hurt her. The gentleman would lie awake at night and stare
the great wink down, would make his pallet on the book of
hurts, and if Jack tried to slither out from among his pages and
between her sheets, he'd be taken by the eye, blinded for good
and all.

If these be lies, they are but slight distortion. The gentleman will
do the things he can: chop down the stalk or lay the golden
egg, be the harp that sings. Or he will wink and blind her with
his love.

THE PORTRAIT OF A CLOWN

Which way will he go
 for his lips
are at the edge of something

shades of blue rose-flushed
 it is a
pavilion on the green wall silk

and canvas and the wall
 is on the
edge of something the room is

hanging on the lip of
 evening neither starward
nor sunward how will the clown

maintain his equipoise as a
 world as a
room tips the frame tilts shades

of aquamarine the bold lines
 of a face
ride over the sleeping child.

"The Shelves"   *collagraph*

THE STUDY

The lamp is standing in the corner of the study: a tree with a crown
of light rises out of the braided rug.

The Inhabitant's books form two walls which rise, like the voices of
a thousand men, two-thirds of the way toward the tall ceiling.

He is not thinking of poems under cover, of periodicals with pages
curling like leaves under fall trees. The Inhabitant is watching
the lamp, for it is a tree which puts forth beams instead of
limbs.

The tree leans away from its source. Its eccentricity is that of
bias.

This is the Inhabitant's room; he shares it, for the moment, with
Corelli and the lamp, but the study falls away from the bole,
as the Inhabitant has fallen away from his pages and his youth.
The lamp keeps the chairs and shelves from flying too far from
an axis.

Behind the shading fabric there are filaments which flame at a touch.
The tree in its foliage burns at the center of things.

This is where the Inhabitant lives. These things are his — these
books, this music upon which the lamplight falls, upon which
he too, once, threw a radiance now eaten by wires tapping the
sources of silence and desuetude.

The lamp, rising out of the study's braided rug, keeps the Inhabitant
from flying too far beyond peripheries. Light, he muses, uses
oddly the things we use.

THE CAT

Long-haired and black as shadow
the cat comes to drive
a pad of yellow foolscap
and a ballpoint pen out

of the Inhabitant's hands for
it is time again to
handle the palpable dark not
to compose to write about

the loom and shuttle of
shadow moving mechanically across clock
faces but to pass hands
lightly down the pelt of

smooth moments look you no
harm is meant by this
passage it is just that
things were meant to be

this way the waiting the
soft animal with sharp teeth
and claws sheathed lurking in
corners will come out to

be stroked and enjoyed for
it is lethal but sensual
as well and it means
no particular ill the hour

for striking has not arrived
it is not the enemy
but a familiar of houses
a domestic that keeps accounts.

"THE BED"

"The Bed"   *etching*

THE BEDROOM

*(An adaptation from the French of Yves Bonnefoy's
"A Shadow Breathing")*

The mirror on the morning wall listens as swelling waters speak
darkly across the room. Two beacons converge and blend
among drifting lamps and tables.

The Inhabitant is an island of somnolence adrift, melding with
another along stone borders where the placid seas of dream are
lost — forever shaped, forever shattered. A current stirs in the
vague depth of dream, and, distantly, upon the darker water
of a table, the red dress, burning, sleeps.

It was midnight long ago; a static star ordered the spirals of other
suns. Night's original hour bore noons in its lumen, and words
were whispered into the foliage of darkness:

An indifferent star, a ship's mast — the clear trail of one or the other
in still waters and firmament: whatever is stirred like a vessel
which turns, which glides, which does not know its own heart
in the night.

They have this sleep to traverse, like an immense, immobile sea,
the Inhabitant's lone consciousness becoming eyes, mouth, and
heart of the vessel's mast, loving the dark currents, drinking her
eyes without memories. He was without that dream of absences
which grasp and do not grasp, wishless to keep her midnight
hues: blue and stone, magnificent, where nothing ever ends.

Waters of the sleeper, tree of absence, hours without beaches; in that
boundlessness a night begins to end. How shall the Inhabitant
name the new day — this muted mixture of crimson and sable?

In the sleepers' eyes beacons dim. Words are minted which begin to disperse the night's sparks, obscuring stars in the spindrift of meaning — it is nearly the moment of waking, already remembrance.

The Inhabitant does not know how to sleep without her; he does not dare risk without her this motionless progression. Too late he has found it to be one more dream — this region of compasses tumbling toward death.

He has wished her, on his fever's pillow, not to be — or to be dark as the clock's shadow. Yet when he spoke aloud in the empty planet, she was there on sleep's vast seaways.

Dreams urged him on — dreams illuminated with vagrant lamps. Night after night her reflection kept him from edges — darknesses beyond darkness . . . dawn and morning love.

The Inhabitant bent to that vale of numberless stones, listened to its grave repose. He perceived, covert among gigantic shades, the grotto where sleep's spindrift bleaches.

He listened to dream — monotonous, hollow, now and then shattered by blind rock. Her voice faded, overwhelmed by darkness; yet a freshet of narrow hope murmured in the desert.

Elsewhere, in lustrous gardens, the Inhabitant knows it is true: a pagan peacock flaunts its mortal raiment. But his single beacon suffices for her! She clothes the night with a curved phrase.

Who is she? He knows her only as alarums, as a voice urging haste in an unfinished rite. She apportions darkness to a tabletop — her eyes like suns, the only lights.

THE PILLOW

It is stuffed with
    dreams children swim
unborn among feathers their eyes

    hooded spools rolling threads
        unwinding among the
    wrinkled hands here and now

    there raveling the moon
        falling through the
    window white light the hardness

    of bone needling fabric
        stitching no time
    into a patchwork darkness it

        is the stuff of
            sleep and wish
    turning ghosts into children children

        to phantoms touching out
            of soft darkness
    for moonlight and unreachable time.

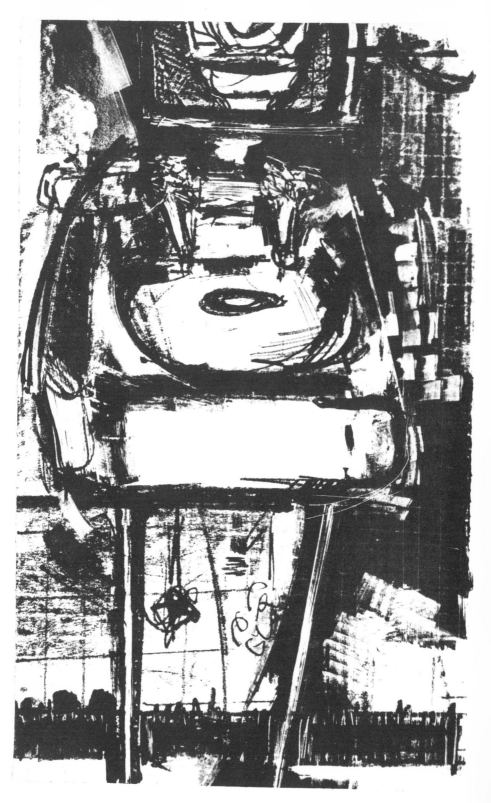

"The Sink"   *lithograph*

THE BATHROOM

He will wash away the dross of sleep in the thin room made of
porcelain and tile. The Inhabitant will emerge another man —
the old one will diminish in steam and water hissing or bubbling
in taps and bowls.

The effluvia of dream will become the vapors of waking. Blades
scrape away the night's stubble — those excrescences blood
pushes through flesh when no one is watching.

Liquid needles spurt at his shoulderblades, turn to spume under
brisk hands. The drain sucks and gargles, swallowing sleep.

The nap and pile of toweling, with ten thousand small tongues, lick
the body dry. In the mirror, under the comb's teeth, an efful-
gence emerges to gleam back at gaze.

Bristles and wax. Now the instar appears, palpitant in the steamy
light of another morning breaking through the frosted glass.

THE MIRROR

In the mirror this
other the heart of glass
brave beyond
his agate eyes

in them currents forever
at their gaze look away
catch him
at a glance

this creature of mercury
make him stop staring out
of himself
into crystal so

clear so foretelling that
he can surely see floating
in shallows
the shoddy heart.

"THE BASEMENT"

detail from "The House" *Basement*

THE BASEMENT

The Inhabitant descends to find the child's lost doll. The door, the narrow stair, the snaky mop on sentry at the stairhead — these have been managed.

The light here is yellow; the walls drink its treacle, turn it to cobwebbing and dust, a faint odor of coal left over from another year.

The walls drink sound as well — the Inhabitant's thin whistle, the squeal of the furnace flywheel turning, saying small things, informing the spider's fretwork of minuscule agonies. The voice of a mouse is strapped to silence spinning.

Beside the set-tubs the toys lie in their boxes. In the sinks, stagnant water ebbs and tides, the curved hose of the washer arches downward, but never touches the surface — never quite touches the grey surface rising and falling in the clogged pipes, the storm drains under the cellar leading outward and downward.

The Inhabitant will find her, must find her for the yearning child. She will be in the boxes, clothed in rags, wearing her painted smile and a scraped eye, its metal beginning to corrode.

His fingers brush through the castoff things: some blocks, a partial deck of minicards — King of Spades and Queen of Hearts —, Pinocchio without his rubber nose. The toys drift in the dusk like the buoys of time, shadowmarks on darkness.

Upstairs the child is waiting, having remembered, wanting the past as palpable as chain. But this is carrying water in a sieve: a toy boat rides with a ragged sail, adrift, its anchor dragging through the dust like stars.

Here she lies at last, the lost toy in her apron, smiling like yarn out of the yawning box. Take her and carry her to the stair as the wheel stands still, the tides lie quiet in the soapy tubs; do not glance back nor at the ragged doll or she shall be left at the stairhead beneath the writhing mop, and the wheel will begin to spin, its voice to whine — the webs will net dust in the billowing corners when night '

P. 47, last stanza, last line: "when the light goes out," not "when night goes out."

THE SCYTHE

The crescent blade with its snake
handle hangs on the cellar
wall waiting for another
day like last
summer's milkweed
day

when the bees in the great patch
of blossoms out back made
an electric sound as
the Inhabitant came
out to
whittle

the congregation of stalks into
a large circle then slowly
a smaller one scything
in spirals the
bees moving
always

toward the center as the ring
of petal and stamen contracted
the stalks falling bleeding
milk as the
crescent edge
stroked

in passing and the buzzing thickened
at heart until only a
last fist of milkweed
stood crowned with
bees drinking
one

nightcap of nectar before dusk cut
into the still green air
and the Inhabitant leaned
on the snake
against his
blade.

"THE PORCH"

detail from "The House" *Porch*

THE PORCH

It was a quiet June evening; therefore, the noise of the collision reached across the green yards and caught the Inhabitant listening to the tickings a porch makes.

It was this evening, and he was filing cards in a mailing list; he could not sleep — it was yesterday, and the names on their white rectangles sifted through his fingers.

He ran, and the neighbors ran, collecting at the corner; therefore, six-score eyes peered into the road at the spectacle.

Before the sound there had been another sound. A siren, on this street of sirens, coming close, wiring the afternoon — stitching it with steel to the approaching darkness.

In the road — the automobile, the woman fainting at the wheel, the left fender smashed. The windshield of the car cast a spiderweb against the sun.

An ambulance, spun into the curb opposite, nosed against the grass as though it were a steel beast grazing; therefore, the doors at its rear gaped open before the crowd who could see the dying man:

Like cardboard, he lay on the floor where he had fallen. His stiff frame littered the collision.

The attendants wrestled with time; therefore, his bones gave to their ministrations, swelling the shrunken flesh, lying at last upon the stretcher in the center of the street.

It was a dead man, the hair grown long upon his parchment scalp. Or perhaps it was a woman, barely breathing, her accident compounded, her body diminished by a thousand thousand accidents of moment.

They stared at the creature; a child cried, "See his bones!" Therefore its mother said, "Hush," and the spectators listened to each other babbling, but heard nothing more than their silent periphrasis.

They helped the first woman, weeping, from her car. She had been forgotten, but now she walked with help toward the hospital nearby, past the prime cause who never had awakened, who never knew he or she had been thrown down, who lay like a sacks of winter in the center of a summer street.

The body must be moved; therefore, a passing mail truck stopped, came backing down the street; its grate gaped open to receive the late delivery.

Now it is gone; the neighbors stand and talk, their voices sharp with fright, but tongues blunted with relief. The Inhabitant speaks with Mr. Smith until, at last, the failing light disperses the folk as though by accident, diminishes their number interminably.

Some of the crowd will dream; therefore, the Inhabitant shall stay awake upon the porch to work by lamplight upon his cards — ordering his neighbors' names, memorizing the streets of towns, listening to June bloom again and to a cat greeting another dawn.

THE GLIDER

Under Orion nothing
except the glider supported
by the night creaking like
chains and crickets in the yard

remnants of daylight
lie glittering or is
it dew or stars fallen
or warnings of dawn no matter

for now the
glider vessel of summer
first starship insubstantial as
its voyages enters the wind even

as the evening
is mild scented with
lilac enters winter wheels in
starlight which rimes the glider chains

crickets the night
and suddenly the silence
which settles darkly among the
lawn's glitterings for this briefest moment.

P. 52, first stanza, last line:
"sack of winter," not "sacks."

THE GUESTROOM

The Inhabitant must go around thinking of Death. Have at him, call him fool and scofflaw — he will think of Death.

There is a room where an old man lies dreaming of worms. In the moments of his eyes all the world is buried: its fables and laces are spread like tablecloths for his sons to walk on.

The feast is laid; he is watched.

He cannot stir without moving earth and water, he cannot sing without upsetting cities, he cannot tap his headboard with a hard white nail without bringing the heavens down, he cannot wink, for there would be avalanches. The Inhabitant dreams of Death, an old man who has many sons.

His daughters are the harvesters of worms. With their quick eyes they watch that there shall be no movement — no grain shall shift unless shifted by river or wind.

There will be life, they say, but life must have its color and shape, and the color we choose is brown, the shape vulgar and thin, a needle of flesh burrowing in flesh. There will be life, they say, but Death must have no mate.

Come with the Inhabitant to see the old man's stone. On it there are graven these words: *Le visage de mon Dieu est calme.*

His daughters have made his epitaph in their language, with their soft hands. They stand and watch in dark garments — no one may change their rune, for their god would tremble in Her fury.

The Inhabitant speaks of a guest who has many sons. His daughters stand on his mouth, weeping and weighting the earth.

THE LOOKING-GLASS

Once in a while
   the eye

circles like a hawk
   comes down

in a place never
   inhabited by

anything animate anything sharp
   or whole

and there lying in
   its circle

of smooth things the
   eye preens

in its own vision
   before it

rakes the wind again
   and rises

into the sun the
   fierce air.

"THE STOVE"

"The Stove"   *collagraph — etching*

THE SUMMERHOUSE

The gazebo looks at summer with the Inhabitant's eyes. The iris blossoms have fallen with spring, and the stalks stand naked now in the night which has gathered-in the house, the summerhouse, the lawn with its banks and peatbeds, the man standing in the darker shadows of his walls.

The Inhabitant's hands take the rough logs of the rail, and he leans to look toward the lighted windows. He grasps the round wood to see into lamplight shining through clear glass.

Inside, the woman moves across the curtains, holding her child drowsy with bedtime. They are netted, kept in gauze, their movements luminous and aquatic.

The air indoors is still and warm. The plants stand at the screens, incline toward the cool darkness where a light breeze, filled with dew, moves over the grass toward the round building in the garden.

They are real, the Inhabitant is thinking, if only for the moment. The grain and knots of the rail hurt his flesh, but he will not shift his stance, for the small pain is good under the indelible wheeling of stars beyond the roof, too far to dream of touching, too near to ignore.

This is what there is. It is enough: the nightwind, the windows alight in the livingroom, the flowers of the garden touching toward the summerhouse, the neighbors on their porches, the road rolling outward into the darkness under streetlamps moth-haloed and the nighthawk's wing and call.

THE GARDEN

Take two
words then three
touch four words make

earrings for
the hearing a
necklace of the snake

in Eve's
garden the apple
of Adam's eye take

two words
touch them join
the leaf and the

twig again
stand naked in
the sun and the

shading branch
in that garden
again wearing only these

the tongue's
jewels the ear's
riches eyes like amethyst.

"THE HOUSE"

THE DWELLING-HOUSE

I.   On the morning of the first day the Inhabitant awoke and went out; he uncoiled the sheets of his dream and walked through the door into a blue sky hung with flowers.

In the streets of his city there moved good people. Men in love with women went quietly among children, and birds settled out of the air to light the parks with their wings.

He looked about him and saw that things were in their places — the trees made figures of light and shadow, their roots matching in the earth the patterns of limbs against the sun.

II.   On the second day it was harder to lose the dream; it had shackles, it seemed, but at last the Inhabitant fought free and woke.

Outdoors the same blue sky, but edged with grey. The color of the air had not changed, but its tone was strange.

The eyes of the men regarded their women as before, gazes placid and assured. brows smooth and cheeks unlined.

Children, among the park paths, fed the winged creatures. The heads of the birds jerked and pecked at crumbs held steadily in small hands.

There was a light wind among the trees, whose leaves sometimes showed white undersides to the breathing air.

III.   The dream stayed with him on the third day. The Inhabitant had trouble unwinding the night, and there were strange images attending him to the door.

A tree grew out of his doorstep, grey ribbons tangled in its branches. A trunk of steel sprung upward, and an explosion of metal limbs groped the sky.

The men on the streets stood rigidly with the women, and the children watched. The fathers were staring, only their eyes alive, at the mothers standing among their offspring.

Wings were spread unmoving in the wind; in the parks the pigeons were frozen in the air among the vines that grew upward toward them.

But at last he blinked, and the dream was gone. The city hidden behind the veil emerged and moved upon him.

IV.   His eyes were the door itself when the fourth day broke. The Inhabitant's lids opened and the black sun shone into his dream.

From the steel tree that pierced his pupils hung the world's fruit: staring out of the husks of their flesh — the eyes of neuter things, men, women and children.

Birds fed upon them. The heads of the plated things hunched and nodded, the sharp beaks piercing the people's eyes.

But the fruit was not diminished. Upon the limbs of the tree of steel the limbs of flesh multiplied and pressed upon each other.

The parks were merged in a garden of vines. The earth twisted upward like hair, each filament coiling toward the suspended folk, touching and holding.

V.   On the fifth day the Inhabitant awoke and saw that God was dead. Silence invested the garden and the star-infested sky.

VI.   On the sixth day he knew he had slept without dreaming. Behind him the night lay empty, like the cold sheets that smoothened about him, above and below.

But the Inhabitant lay with his eyes closed for as long as he could bear, until he sank into the darkness of his mind. No time seeped between his lids, but his vigil was eternal until sleep took him down once again.

VII.   On the morning of the seventh day he woke and arose. In at the window the dawn blew as he stood and looked.

On his legs each hair stood in its chill; he felt the morning moving on his flesh.

In the mirror he saw a man. Upon the surface of the glass there shimmered the image of someone strange and real, bearded, the bone hung with blood's fabric.

He went to the door, naked; opened it; moved into the daylight where the world walked. With his eyes he met other eyes beyond the portal — men, women, and children who knew his nakedness as he knew theirs.

It was a true flesh the Inhabitant made to walk through the city: in each eye he saw the image folk saw in his.